YOUNG ZOOLOGIST
GIANT PANDA

A FIRST FIELD GUIDE TO THE
BAMBOO-LOVING BEAR FROM CHINA

NEON  SQUID

CONTENTS

HELLO, YOUNG ZOOLOGIST!

Welcome to the exciting world of giant pandas! These black-and-white bears are a symbol for conservation around the world and a national treasure in their home country of China. For many years not much was known about these mysterious creatures because they are shy and avoid people on the mountains they call home. But in the last few decades scientists have learned so much about giant pandas from studying them closely. In this book I invite you to discover what makes giant pandas so special. I started learning about these bears when I was six years old—and now I am a giant panda scientist. If you like animals, you could become a scientist who studies them too. Let's get started!

VANESSA HULL

FACT FILE

SCIENTIFIC NAME
Ailuropoda melanoleuca

TYPE
Mammal

ORDER
Carnivores

FAMILY
Bears

HEIGHT
28–31 in
(70–80 cm)

WEIGHT
220–265 lb
(100–120 kg)

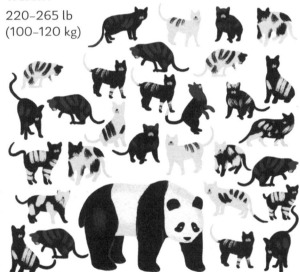

That's about the same as 29 house cats.

LOCATION
Southwest China

HABITAT
Forests

EATS
Bamboo

LIFE SPAN
20 years

CONSERVATION STATUS
Vulnerable

BEFORE YOU GET STARTED

1
2
3
4

1 WET WEATHER GEAR

It can be rainy or snowy in panda habitat, so it is best to be prepared for any weather that might come your way. A nice pair of waterproof boots and an all-weather jacket are a must!

2 CAMERA

You'll want to take photos of anything interesting you see in the mountains—from scratch marks and dung to panda tracks. Don't forget your camera or something you can take photos with, like a phone. Make sure you have spare batteries or a charger.

3 NOTEBOOK & PEN

A notebook is one of a zoologist's most useful tools. It's really important to write down all of the things you observe out in the wild. You need a record of your observations and measurements so you can analyze them when you get home.

Pack your knapsack and get ready to hike into panda habitat! You never know what you might encounter, so it's best to be prepared. Here are some useful items you should have with you before you head out on your adventure.

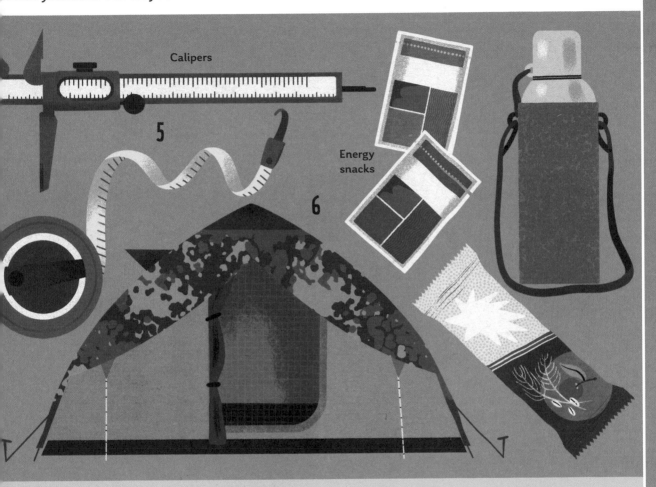

Calipers

Energy snacks

5

6

4 GPS TRACKER

A GPS (Global Positioning System) tracker is also a must. This tool lets you record your location with the help of satellites in space! You can use it to navigate so you don't get lost. It also helps you mark on a map where you made your observations.

5 MEASURING EQUIPMENT

You will need a few different kinds of measuring equipment. Tape measures can be used to calculate the size of animal tracks, trees, or shrubs. For more tricky jobs, like measuring the width of bamboo stems, calipers would be better.

6 TENT & SUPPLIES

You might want to camp out overnight in the woods, so make sure you have your tent and a sleeping bag. Also bring plenty of food, including energy bars, and water to keep you going on the long hike.

MEET THE GIANT PANDA

Because giant pandas live in remote forests in China, they can be hard for scientists to study in the wild. As a result there is still much to learn about these mysterious mammals.

BLACK AND WHITE

Pandas are known for their black-and-white coloration, but it isn't just to make them look pretty! Their black eye patches and black ears stand out against white snow, helping pandas see one another and communicate.

PIGEON TOES

Pandas have "pigeon toes"that point inward. This means that pandas are not fast runners! Luckily they have no natural predators.

THICK FUR

Giant pandas have thick fur that keeps them warm in the cold winter months.

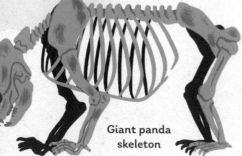

Giant panda skeleton

IN THE FAMILY

Giant pandas are members of the Ursidae family—better known to you and me as bears! They are also closely related to red pandas and raccoons.

BEARS

Brown bear
(Europe, Asia, and North America)

Polar bear
(The Arctic)

Asiatic black bear
(Asia)

American black bear
(North America)

Sun bear
(Southeast Asia)

Sloth bear
(Indian subcontinent)

OTHER RELATIVES

Spectacled bear
(South America)

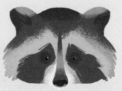

Raccoon
(North America)

Red panda
(Asia)

HOME SWEET HOME

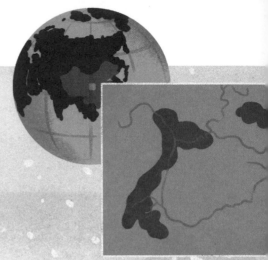

The area where an animal lives is called its habitat. A habitat contains all of the key resources that an animal needs to survive, including food and water. Panda habitat is in the southwest part of China, a country in Asia. The place where pandas live is made up of beautiful forests perched on the sides of mountains.

SMALL AREA

Panda habitat is incredibly small. There are only five mountain ranges (the red areas on the map above) where pandas live in the wild.

FRIENDLY FOREST

There are lots of trees in panda habitat. A healthy forest is important for pandas because it helps support the growth of bamboo, the panda's main food.

Pandas like to climb trees so they can enjoy the sunshine.

STEEP MOUNTAIN

The mountains where pandas live are very steep and get a lot of snow in winter. It is sometimes hard for people to climb the mountains, but pandas are great at it!

THIRSTY WORK

There are many rivers in panda habitat. They bring water from the high peaks of the mountains down to the valleys below. Pandas will head to a river every day to drink.

BAMBOO

Pandas mainly eat bamboo, a woody plant in the grass family. And they eat *a lot* of it. Instead of eating three meals a day, they eat bamboo throughout the day and night. They can't get enough of it!

THUMBS-UP

Pandas have a sixth digit on each of their front paws. It is called a "pseudo-thumb," and it helps them grip bamboo while they are eating.

TUMMY MICROBES

Pandas have tiny organisms called microbes in their stomach. These special helpers allow them to digest, or break down, bamboo. Pandas wouldn't be able to eat bamboo without them.

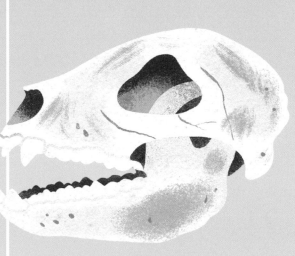

TAKE YOUR PICK

Pandas eat many different types of bamboo. Some are thick and as tall as a person, while others are short and thin. Pandas eat all parts of bamboo—the stem, the leaves, and the branches.

SPECIAL GNASHERS

Long ago, pandas were carnivores (meat eaters), but over time they evolved to mostly eat bamboo. Their back teeth, called molars, are large and wide. This helps them chew the tough bamboo stems.

BAMBOO POOP

Pandas poop up to 40 times a day! That's what happens when you're not very good at digesting bamboo and you eat constantly. If you ever come face-to-face with panda poop in real life, look closely. You should be able to see leaves and stems.

DAILY ACTIVITIES

By studying pandas, scientists have gotten to know their daily habits well. Each day is filled with activities they perform in order to survive. And two in particular take up most of their time...

NAP TIME (43%)

Pandas need lots of sleep. They snooze for eight to twelve hours a day. They sleep during both day and night, usually in naps lasting two to three hours. They love napping in trees while they enjoy the sunshine.

WALKING (3%)

Pandas walk from one place to another, usually to find the next bamboo patch. But they don't need to walk very far—bamboo is all around them!

GPS TRACKER

Scientists have learned how pandas spend their day by putting GPS collars on their necks. The collar doesn't hurt the panda. It transmits signals to satellites, telling us the panda's location all through the day.

EATING (50%)

Pandas spend much of their day eating—from 12 to 14 hours a day! When they eat they like to sit down and relax inside a bamboo patch so they can easily reach for the bamboo all around them.

OTHER (4%)

The rest of the time pandas dedicate to drinking water and finding mates. Mother pandas also spend time caring for their young cubs.

ON THE MOVE

DOWN IN THE VALLEYS

In some parts of panda habitat, there is a very tasty bamboo that grows down in the valleys in spring. Pandas will head down the mountain to find this bamboo, then climb back up the mountain afterward.

As we've established, pandas don't like to move too much. However, there is one thing that makes them travel short distances—or migrate—up and down the mountains each year. You guessed it: bamboo!

UP IN THE MOUNTAINS

Some pandas prefer to be on the higher parts of the mountain for the winter and summer. This is where they find their favorite bamboo for these times of the year.

SLEEPY COUSINS

Many bears sleep all winter long. This is called hibernating. When it's cold, there is less food available, so they rest and save their energy before waking up in the spring. But pandas don't hibernate! This is because bamboo doesn't die during the winter, meaning pandas can eat it all through the year.

LEAVING A SCENT

Pandas have a super smart way of communicating with one another: scent marking! They have a gland under their tail that releases a sticky and smelly liquid. They rub this liquid against trees in their habitat. Other pandas come along, smell the scent on the tree, and know who was there before. Pandas use different techniques to leave their scent.

QUADRUPEDAL

In this position the panda keeps all four legs on the ground (that's what "quadrupedal" means). The panda backs up to a tree with its tail raised and rubs back and forth.

Scent marking tells pandas who is ready to mate.

THE LEG COCK

A classic position in which a panda lifts one back leg up on a tree and uses the other back leg for balance.

SQUAT

Squatting allows pandas to leave their scent on the ground or a tree stump. It's also—let's face it—easier than a handstand (see below).

THE HANDSTAND

This pose is used by male pandas. They try to compete to see who can do the tallest handstand and get the highest mark on the tree!

SMELLY WORK

Each scent is unique to the panda that produced it—kind of like a fingerprint. Pandas spend a lot of time alone. They use scent marking to keep track of their panda neighbors from a distance.

MAKE SOME NOISE

1 **BLEAT**
The bleat sounds like the noise a sheep makes. Pandas bleat as a friendly greeting to another panda. The bleat tells us the panda is happy to see its friend!

2 **SQUEAL**
The squeal is a high-pitched sound that pandas make when they are scared. For example, a cub might squeal if it's stuck in a tree. Pandas also squeal if they are hurt, much like humans do.

3 **CHIRP**
If you hear chirping in a forest, it could be a bird—or a panda! Female pandas use this sound if they're worried about their cub, or to tell a male panda that they're interested in mating.

Pandas can make 13 different sounds, and each one has a different meaning. Here are a few of the most common noises. Do you think you can do a good panda impression?

4 HONK
If a panda is worried about something, or upset because it has injured itself, it will make a honking noise. This sounds kind of like a car.

5 BARK
If you thought only dogs barked, think again. Pandas will bark when they sense danger. For example, a panda will bark if it is startled by a hiker.

A CUB'S LIFE

1 **TINY AND PINK**
When they're born the cubs have no fur and are completely blind. Unlike many other bears, mother pandas in the wild only raise one cub at a time. Each cub can get all of the mother's attention!

2 **BLACK AND WHITE**
After about a month pandas start to develop their characteristic black-and-white fur. They no longer look like a pink blob.

3 **HUGS FROM MOM**
Mothers are very important for panda cubs. The cubs drink their mother's milk and stay warm in their fur. The mom even has to rub their bellies to make them poop! Mothers will teach cubs all of the skills they need to survive.

Mothers keep their babies inside a warm den in a cave or large tree for the first few months.

When they're born, panda cubs are completely helpless and require around-the-clock care from their mother. After a few months, these playful cubs are full of mischief and ready for their first climbing lessons.

6 CLIMBING LESSONS
Panda cubs love to climb trees and will start climbing at around six months old. Mother keeps a close eye so the cub won't fall! Panda cubs will stay with their mothers for two years before going off on their own.

4 CRAWLING CUBS
At about ten weeks old the panda cubs start to crawl. They begin to explore their den.

5 SOLID FOOD
Panda cubs get their teeth when they're around 14 weeks old. When they're six months old they start to eat bamboo for the first time!

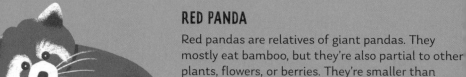

RED PANDA

Red pandas are relatives of giant pandas. They mostly eat bamboo, but they're also partial to other plants, flowers, or berries. They're smaller than giant pandas and look more like raccoons.

Red pandas love to climb trees and sleep in the branches.

NEIGHBORS

Many other animals also live in panda habitat. Pandas don't mind these neighbors because each species eats different things and has different needs. Pandas don't hunt other animals (usually!) and are known for being peaceful neighbors. Let's meet some of the other animals of the forest.

TAKIN

The takin belongs to the same family as sheep and goats. But it is as large as an ox! Takin are known for their sharp horns and stinky, oily hair.

SAMBAR

The sambar is a large deer that eats plants, such as grass and shrubs. The males have big antlers and shaggy hair. Females travel in small groups, while males live alone.

TEMMINCK'S TRAGOPAN

The Temminck's tragopan is one of the many birds in panda habitat. These colorful birds run along the ground looking for plants and berries. The males make loud mating calls.

There are many insects in panda habitat that you can't find anywhere else in the world.

GOLDEN SNUB-NOSED MONKEY

This monkey is an endangered animal that lives in large groups. You can find them in the forest jumping from one tree branch to another as they look for fruits and leaves.

THREATS TO PANDAS

ANCIENT SKULLS

Panda fossils have been found all over China. This tells us that hundreds of years ago, pandas used to live over a huge area that was at least ten times the size of the current panda habitat.

A giant panda skull

Only around 1,800 pandas are left in the wild today.

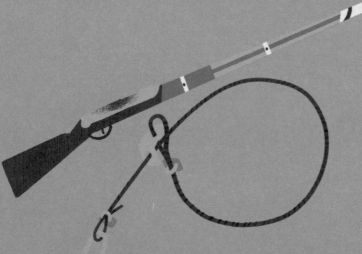

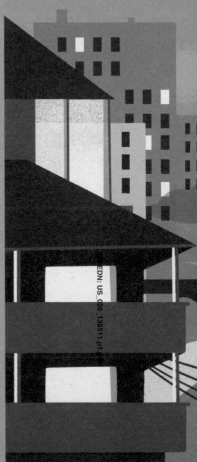

POACHING

Around 30 years ago, poaching was a threat to pandas. They were hunted for their fur. Now there are strict laws against this, so few pandas are killed by hunters today.

Giant pandas face many challenges to survive as a species. This means we need to keep a close eye on the threats they come up against in the wild. Most of the issues are due to the loss or destruction of their habitat.

DEFORESTATION

One of the biggest threats to giant pandas is the destruction of their forest habitat, also known as deforestation. Forests have been cut down to make room for people.

FARMING

Livestock grazing is another threat to pandas. Local farmers raise cows, sheep, and horses. Sometimes they let the animals roam in panda habitat, where they eat and trample bamboo.

CITIES AND ROADS

Panda habitat is broken up into many small pieces because roads and houses have been built between the forests. This makes it hard for pandas to find one another.

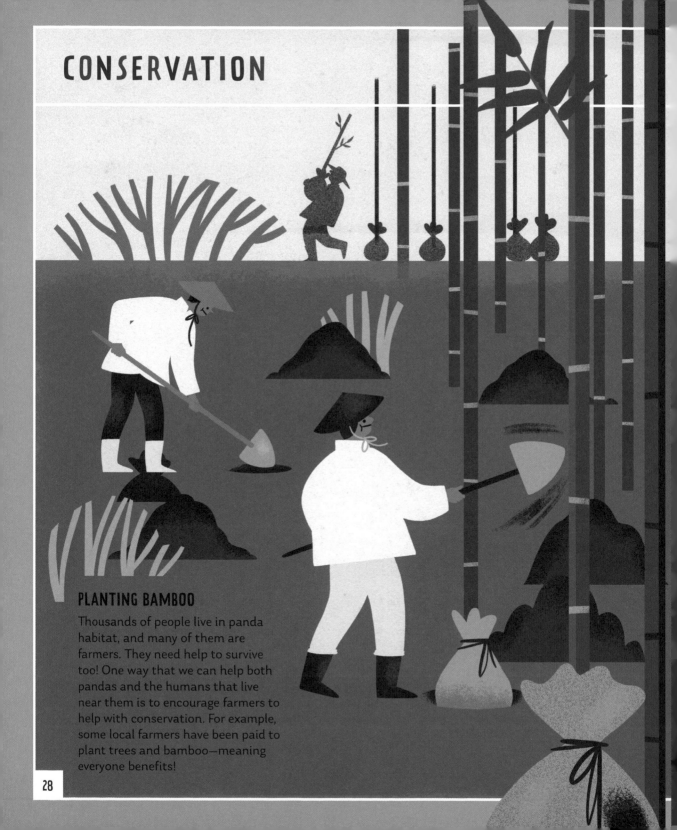

CONSERVATION

PLANTING BAMBOO

Thousands of people live in panda habitat, and many of them are farmers. They need help to survive too! One way that we can help both pandas and the humans that live near them is to encourage farmers to help with conservation. For example, some local farmers have been paid to plant trees and bamboo—meaning everyone benefits!

Giant pandas need us to work hard so that they can survive for years to come. We need to keep finding new ways to protect and improve their habitat so they have safe places to call home.

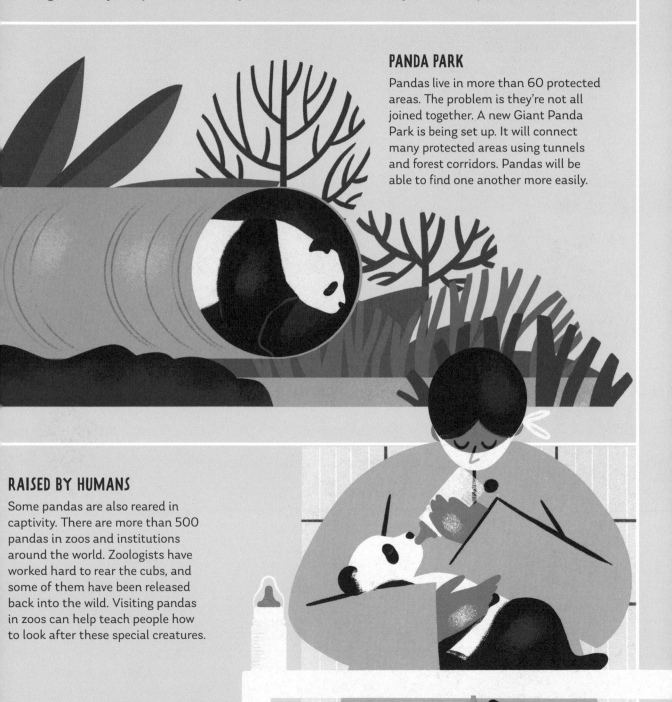

PANDA PARK

Pandas live in more than 60 protected areas. The problem is they're not all joined together. A new Giant Panda Park is being set up. It will connect many protected areas using tunnels and forest corridors. Pandas will be able to find one another more easily.

RAISED BY HUMANS

Some pandas are also reared in captivity. There are more than 500 pandas in zoos and institutions around the world. Zoologists have worked hard to rear the cubs, and some of them have been released back into the wild. Visiting pandas in zoos can help teach people how to look after these special creatures.

GLOSSARY

Bamboo
A plant in the grass family that is the giant panda's main food.

Calipers
A tool used to measure the thickness of bamboo stems.

Carnivore
An animal that eats meat. Pandas were originally carnivores, but over time they evolved to eat bamboo.

Conservation
Actions that people take to protect animals and the environment.

Deforestation
The act of cutting down a large area of trees.

Den
A safe place where a mother panda gives birth and rears her cub—usually a tree or cave.

GPS collar
A tool put around an animal's neck to track its location and see where it travels over time. GPS stands for "Global Positioning System."

Habitat
The place where an animal lives, including all of the resources in that place that the animal needs to survive—such as food and water.

Herbivore
An animal that eats plants.

Hibernation
Some animals rest, or hibernate, during winter. Hibernation is important for saving energy when there is less food around.

Mammal
A type of animal that produces milk to look after its young. Pandas and humans are both mammals.

Poaching
The illegal killing of an animal that is protected.

Predator
An animal that eats by killing other animals.

Prey
An animal that is eaten by other animals.

Protected areas
Special areas that are set up with the goal of keeping wildlife safe.

Pseudo-thumb
The long wrist bone that pandas have that works just like a thumb, helping them grip bamboo stems.

Scent marking
When a panda spreads a smelly, sticky liquid on a surface like a tree to communicate with other pandas.

Zoologist
A scientist who studies animals.

INDEX

This has been a

NEON  SQUID

production

For Haru and Nari

Author: Vanessa Hull
Illustrator: Charlotte Molas
US Editor: Allison Singer

Neon Squid would like to thank:

Jane Simmonds for proofreading.

Copyright © 2022
St. Martin's Press
120 Broadway, New York,
NY 10271

Created for St. Martin's Press by
Neon Squid
The Stables, 4 Crinan Street,
London, N1 9XW

EU representative: Macmillan
Publishers Ireland Ltd,
1st Floor, The Liffey Trust Centre,
117–126 Sheriff Street Upper,
Dublin 1, D01 YC43

10 9 8 7 6 5 4 3 2 1

The right of Vanessa Hull to be identified as the author of this work has been asserted in accordance with the Copyright, Designs and Patents Act, 1988.

Library of Congress Cataloging-in-Publication Data is available.

Printed and bound by
Vivar Printing in Malaysia.

ISBN: 978-1-684-49221-3

Published in June 2022.

www.neonsquidbooks.com